"Happy Hours" at the Newsroom Jazz Club

Ted Carelock

Party Jokes

Adult Humor

Why There Are No Black Folks in Hell

Funny as Hell

Me Too

No Race Is Safe

No-Fault Sex Contract

Dirty Office Memos

"HAPPY HOURS" AT THE NEWSROOM JAZZ CLUB

iUniverse books may be ordered through booksellers or by contacting:

iUniverse
1663 Liberty Drive
Bloomington, IN 47403
www.iuniverse.com
844-349-9409

ISBN: 978-1-6632-5001-8 (sc)
ISBN: 978-1-6632-5002-5 (e)

Library of Congress Control Number: 2023901067

Print information available on the last page.

iUniverse rev. date: 01/30/2023

I would like a special thanks to my beautiful and caring wife Deanie (Alcoser) Carelock, to my beautiful daughter, Janine Jude. Rev .Theodore Miller for his prayers and inspiration. I also like to thank Seynabou for her excellent typing job.

Thank you to all of my customers and making The News Room Jazz a special "GO TO" place in New York. Special thanks to my dad (hell of a fun guy), mother, sister Gail, and to my cousin Hoyte Sr. "I listened".

Contents

Introduction

This book is a fun-filled, though sometimes serious collection of jokes, poems, memos, and so on collected while I was the owner of three bars/restaurants in the New York City area. I named the series of bars The News Room Sports Bar and Jazz Club. I did so because of my journalism background and location of two of the bars in the Yankee Stadium area and municipal court building. The News Room Sports Bar was like no other bar/club in the area. It had all sorts of entertainment every night of the week. The bar/club had live jazz bands, poetry readings, and was the first in the area to promote karaoke and crab nights. According to the *Village Voice* newspaper, it had, "the best R&B jukebox in New York," and was called the, "best bar for Yankee rain delay games." (See article on page 00.) Most of the material in the book came from these events.

My customers were from all over the New York area. Off-duty officers, court personnel, correction officers, and Yankee fans, were among those who frequented the club. It was said that Yankee great Babe Ruth (see picture) dropped in back in the old days when the bar first opened. Rumor has it that Jackie Robinson owned the real estate where the original, long-standing News Room Sports Bar was located.

During the shooting of Spike Lee's movie *Summer of Sam,* players such as Mickey Rivers, Reggie Jackson, and Willie Randolph stopped in the club. Other movies filmed in the News Room Sports Bar were *South Paw*, featuring Jake Gyllenhaal and 50 Cent, and *The House That Jack Built*, in which I was featured.

These pages are from a humorous collection of adult underground jokes and office memos. There are a few poems collected from poetry nights at the club. There is a poem from my daughter, Janine Carelock, as a tribute to 9/11. A good friend, neighbor, and customer was killed in the Twin Towers that tragic day. I hope you find these jokes and memos humorous and enjoyable and will laugh as much as I did. If you like this book, so will your friends. Send a copy of this book as a gift to your favorite person.

If you say it can't be done,
You're right; it can't be done.

—Ted Carelock

Success Requires Some Effort

—Ted Carelock

JOKES

SOMEBODY

TED CARELOCK

Black Folks in Heaven

Gabriel came to the Lord and said, "I have to talk to you. I have Black folks up here in heaven who are causing some problems.

"They are swinging on the pearly gates, my horn is missing, barbecue sauce is all over their robes, and ham hocks, chicken, spareribs, and pigs' feet bones are all over the streets of gold. Some folks are walking around with one wing. They have been late taking their turns in keeping the stairway to heaven clean. There are watermelon seeds all over the clouds. Some of them aren't even wearing their halos, saying it is messin' up their hair."

The Lord said, "I made them special as I did you, my angel. Heaven is home to all my children. If you really want to know about problems, let's call the devil."

The devil answered the phone. "Hello? Dang, hold on." The devil returned to the phone and said, "Hello, Lord. What can I do for you?"

The Lord replied, "Tell me what kind of problems you are having down there."

The devil said, "Wait one minute," and put the Lord on hold. After five minutes, he returned to the phone, and said, "Okay, I'm back. What was the question?"

The Lord said, "What kind of problems are you having down there?"

The devil said, "Man, I don't belie … Hold on, Lord."

This time the devil was gone for fifteen minutes. The devil returned and said, "I'm sorry, Lord, I can't talk right now. These black folks dun put the fire out and are trying to install air-conditioning!"

Jesus Christ is our only salvation.
God bless you always.

No Cussin' in Church

A crusty old man walks into the local Lutheran church and says to the secretary, "I would like to join this damn church."

The astonished woman replies, "I beg your pardon, sir. I must have misunderstood you. What did you say?"

"Listen up, damn it. I said I want to join this damn church!"

"I am very sorry, sir, but that kind of language is not tolerated in our church."

The secretary leaves her desk and goes into the pastor's study to inform him of the situation. The pastor agrees that the secretary does not have to listen to that kind of language.

They both return to her office, and the pastor asks the old geezer, "Sir, what seems to be the problem here?"

"There is no damn problem," the man says. "I just won 200 million bucks in a lottery and want to join this damn church to get rid of some of the money."

Says the pastor, "Is this bitch giving you hard time?"

Was the Night before Christmas—Ghetto Version

Was the night before Christmas,
When all through the house,
Everybody felt shitty.
Hell, even the mouse.

Tom at the whorehouse,
Dad smoking grass,
I'd just settled down
For a nice piece of ass.

Then out on the lawn
I heard such a clatter,
So I spring from my bed
To see what was the matter.

Then out on the lawn
I saw a big dick.
Knew right away
It must be St. Nick.

He came down the chimney
Like a bat out of hell.
I knew in a moment
The fucker had fell.

He filled all our stockings
With pretzels and beer,
And big rubber dick
For my cousin the queer.

Then he rose up the chimney
With a thunderous fart.
That fat son of a bitch
Blew the chimney apart.

He swore and he cursed
As he rode out of sight,
"Piss on you all,
And have a hell of a night."

Christmas in the Hood

It was the night before Christmas,
when all through the house,
the whole damn family was drunk
as a louse.
Grandpa and Grandma were singing
a song,
and the kid was in bed flogging
his dong.

Ma, home from the cathouse,
and I out of jail had just settled
down for a good piece of tail.
When out on the lawn there arose
such a clatter,
I jumped off Ma to see what was
the matter.

Away to the window I made a mad dash,
threw open the window, and fell on my
ass.
And what to my bloodshot eyes should
appear,
but a rusty old driver sleigh and a dozen
reindeer.

With a little old driver holding
his dick,
I knew in a moment the bastard was
Nick.
Slower than snails his chargers they
came.
He bitched and he swore as he called
them by name.

"Now Dancer, now Prancer, up over the
walls.
Hurry, damn it, or I'll cut off your
balls.
Then up on the roof he stumbled and
fell,
and came down the chimney like a bat
out of hell.

He staggered and stumbled and went
to the door.
He tripped on his dick and fell to the floor.
I heard him exclaim as he drove out
Of sight,
"Fuck you all; it's been a hell of a night."

A Foreigner Who Went to New York

One day Ima go to New York to a bigga hotel. I go down to eat soma breakfast. I tella the waitress I wanna two piss toast. She branga me only onea piss. I tella her I wanna two piss. She say, "Go to the toilet."

I say, "You no understand. I wanna two piss on my plate."

She say, "You better no piss on the plate, you sonna ma bitch." I don't even know the lady, and she calla me, "Sonna ma bitch."

Later, I go to eat soma lunch at Drake Restaurant. The waitress bringa me a spoon ana knife but no fock. I tella her I wanna fock. She tellsa me, "Everybody wanna fock."

I tella her, "You no understand. I wanna fock on the table."

She say, "You better not fock on the table, you sonna ma bitch." I don't even know the lady, and she call me a sonna ma bitch.

So I go back to my room inna hotel, and there's no sheet on my bed. I calla the manager ana tell him I wanna sheet. He tells me to go to the toilet. So I say, "You no understand. I wanna sheet on the bed."

He say, "You better not sheet on the bed, you sonna ma bitch." I don't even know the man, ana he call me a sonna ma bitch.

I go to check out, and the man at the desk, he say, "Peace to you."

I say, "Piss onna you, too, you sonna ma bitch."

I go back to Italy!

If You Are Unhappy

Once upon a time, there was a nonconforming sparrow who decided not to fly south for the winter.

However, soon the weather turned so cold that he began to reluctantly start to fly south. In a short time, ice began to form on his wings, and he fell to earth in a barnyard, almost frozen. A cow passed by and crapped on the little sparrow. The sparrow thought I was the end. But the manure warmed him and defrosted his wings. Warm and happy, able to breathe, he started to sing.

Just then, a large cat came by, and hearing the chirping, investigated the sounds. The cat cleared away the manure, found the chirping bird, and promptly ate him.

The moral of the story:

1. Everyone who shits on you is not necessarily your enemy.
2. Everyone who gets you out of the shit is not necessarily your friend.
3. And if you're warm and happy in a pile of shit, keep your mouth shut.

Recipe for Banana Bread:
Home Cooking for Inexperienced Chefs

Ingredients

2 laughing eyes
2 loving arms
2 well-shaped legs
2 firm milk containers
1 fur-lined mixing bowl
1 large banana

Mixing Instructions

1. Look into laughing eyes.
2. Spread well-shaped legs slowly.
3. Squeeze and massage milk containers very well and gently until fur-lined mixing bowl is well greased. Check frequently with middle finger.
4. Add banana, and gently work in and out until well creamed.
5. Cover with nuts and sigh with relief.

Bread is done when banana becomes soft. Be sure to wash mixing utensils. And don't lick the bowl.

Note: If bread starts to rise, *leave town!*

To: All Who Have Recently Purchased or Are about to Purchase a Dog
Re: What Not to Name Your Dog

Everybody who has a dog calls him Rover or Boy. I call mine Sex.

Now, Sex has been very embarrassing to me. When I went to city hall to renew his dog license, I told the clerk I would like to have a license for Sex. He said, "I'd like to have one too."

Then I said, "But this is a dog." He said he didn't care what she looked like. Then I said, "You don't understand. I've had Sex since I was nine years old."

He said, "You must have been quite a kid!"

When I got married and went on my honeymoon, I took the dog with me. I told the hotel clerk that I wanted a room for my wife and me and a special room for Sex. He said that every room in the place was for sex. I said, "You don't understand, Sex keeps me awake at night."

The clerk said, "Me too."

One day I entered Sex in a contest, but before the competition began, the dog ran away. Another contestant asked me why I was just looking around. I told him I had planned to have Sex in the contest. He told me that I should have sold tickets. "But you don't understand," I said. "I had hoped to have Sex on TV." He called me a show-off.

When my wife and I separated, we went to court to fight for custody of the dog. I said, "Your honor, I had Sex before I was married."

TED CARELOCK

The judge said, "Me too." Then I told him that after I was married, Sex left me. He said, "Me too."

Last night Sex ran off again. I spent hours looking around town for him. A cop came over to me and asked, "What are you doing in the alley at 4 o'clock in the morning?"

I said, "I'm looking for sex."

My case comes up Friday.

A Nun, a Priest, and a Camel

A nun, a priest, and a camel were walking in the desert when all of a sudden, the camel dropped to the ground. The nun asked the preacher what they should do. The preacher said, "If you take off your clothes, I'll show you," because being a preacher, he had never seen a naked woman. So she did as she was told.

Then the nun told the preacher to take off his pants because she had never seen a naked man since she was a nun. So he took them off. When the nun saw his penis, she asked, "What's that?"

The preacher replied, "This brings people to life with pleasure."

Then the nun said, "Well, stick it in the camel, and let's get the hell out of here!"

Dying Man and His Cookies

An old man lay in the bed, dying. As he lay there, he smelled his favorite cookies baking. Chocolate chip. So he rolled out of bed, crawled to the landing, and fell down the stairs. He crawled, gasping for breath, to the kitchen and reached on the table for the cookie. He almost had it when his wife came in. She smacked his hand away from the cookie. "W-why d-d-did you d-do that? he gasped.

She replied, "They are for the funeral tomorrow."

The Punk Kid

One day an old guy gets on a bus. Several minutes later, a punk kid with the red, green, and orange hair gets on. The kid notices that the old man keeps staring at him. The kid looks at him and says, "What are you staring at, old man? Ain't you ever done anything wild in your time?"

The old guy replies, "Yeah, I fucked a parrot once. I was just wondering if you were my kid."

Older Women Are Better

Older women have jobs with dental plans. Younger women can't help you when your teeth get knocked out playing hockey.

An older woman will never accuse you of "using her." She's using you.

Older women take charge of the situation. An older woman will call you up and ask you for a date. A younger woman will wait forever by the phone for you to call.

Older women know how to cook. Young women know how to dial Pizza Hut takeout.

An older woman will introduce you to all her girlfriends. A younger woman will avoid her girlfriends when she's with you in case you get any ideas.

Older women are psychic. You never have to confess to having an affair because somehow, they always know.

Older women often own an interesting collection of lingerie that they have acquired from admirers over the years. Young women often don't wear underpants at all, thus practically eliminating all possibility of a striptease.

An older woman will agree to go to McDonald's with you for a meal. Younger women are too nervous to eat anything in front of somebody that they might possibly boff later.

Older women are dignified. They are beyond having a screaming match with you in the middle of the night in a public park.

Older women are experienced. They understand that sometimes after twelve beers, a boy just can't get it up. A younger woman may need some time to grasp this fact.

An older woman has lots of girlfriends, and most of them will want to boff you too.

An older woman will never accuse you of stealing the best years of her youth because chances are, someone else has stolen them first.

Did You Know?

How come wrong numbers are never busy?
Do people in Australia call the rest of the world "up over"? Does that screwdriver belong to Philip?
Can a stupid person be a smart-ass?
Does killing time damage eternity?
Why doesn't Tarzan have a beard?
Why is it called lipstick if you can still move your lips? Why is it that night falls but day breaks? Why is the third hand on the watch called a second hand? Why is it that when you're driving and looking for an address, you turn down the volume on the radio?

Why is lemon juice made with artificial flavor and dishwashing liquid made with real lemons?

Are part-time bandleaders semi-conductors? Can you buy an entire chess set in a pawn shop? Daylight savings time—why are they saving it, and where do they keep it?

Did Noah keep his bees in archives?
Do jellyfish get gas from eating jellybeans? Do pilots take crash courses?
Do stars clean themselves with meteor showers? Do you think that when they asked George Washington for ID that he just whipped out a quarter?

Have you ever imagined a world with no hypothetical situations? Have you ever seen a toad on a toadstool?
How can there be self-help "groups"?
How do you get off a nonstop flight?
How do you write zero in Roman numerals? How many weeks are there in a light-year? If a jogger runs at the speed of sound, can he still hear his Walkman?

Sex Rodeo Style

Two cowboys were sitting in a bar when one asked his friend if he had heard of the new sex position called "rodeo."

His friend said, "No, what is it?"

"Well, you mount your wife from the back, reach around, and cup her breasts with both hands. Then say, 'Boy, those are almost as nice as your sister's.' Then see if you can hold on for eight seconds."

The Rules

The *female* always makes the rules.

The rules are subject to change without notification at any time.

No *male* can possibly know all the rules.

If the *female* suspects the *male* knows all the rules, she must immediately change some or all of the rules.

The *female* is never wrong.

If the *female* is wrong, it is due to a misunderstanding, which was a direct result of something the *male* did or said wrong.

The *male* must immediately apologize for causing said misunderstanding.

The *female* may change her mind at any time.

The *male* must never change his mind without the expressed written consent of the *female*.
The *female* has every right to be angry or upset at any time.

The *male* must remain calm at all times—
unless the *female* wants him to be angry and/or upset.

The *female* must, under no circumstances, let the *male* know whether or not she wants him to be angry and/or upset.

The *male* is expected to read minds at all times.

The *male* who doesn't abide by the rules and can't take the heat lacks a backbone and is a wimp.

Any attempt to document the rules could result in bodily harm.

If the *female* has PMS, all the rules are null and void.

The *female* is ready when she is ready.

The *male* must be ready at all times.

Old Lady and the Penis

Once there was this guy by the name of Kendu who really took care of his body. He lifted weights and jogged six miles every morning. One day, Kendu looked in the mirror to admire his body and noticed that he was suntanned all over with one exception—his penis. He readily decided to do something about it. He went to the beach, undressed, and buried himself in the sand. Well, except for his penis, which he left sticking out.

About this time, two little old ladies strolled by, one using a cane. On seeing the thing sticking out of the sand, she began to move it around, using her cane as she remarked to the other little old lady, "There really is no justice in this world."

The other old lady asked, "What do you mean by that?"

The first old lady replied, "Look at it this way. When I was twenty, I was curious about it. When I was thirty, I enjoyed it. When I was forty, I asked for it. When I was fifty, I paid for it. When I was sixty, I prayed for it. When I was seventy, I forgot about it. And now that I'm eighty, the damn things are growing wild, And I'm too old to squat."

Safety First Guarantee

This certifies that I, the undersigned female,

About to enjoy sexual intercourse with_____, am of the law for age of consent, am in my right mind, and am not under the influence of any drug or narcotic. Nor does he have to use any force, threats, or promises to influence me.

I am in no fear of him whatsoever, do not expect or want to marry him, don't know whether he is married or not, and don't care. I am not asleep or drunk. I am entering into this relation with him because I love it and want it as much as he does, and if I receive the satisfaction I expect, I am very willing to play in an early return engagement.

Furthermore, I agree never to appear as a witness against him or to prosecute under the Mann White-Slave Traffic Act.

Signed before jumping into bed this _____ day of _____, 19____.

Witness my hand and see you:

By _____

Address _____

The Comedy Column

Oh husband, oh husband,
    I tremble with fear.
You've been on the night shift
    for nearly 7 months,
And since you are gone
    all through the night,
A real piece of ass
    seems way out of sight.

Oh husband, dear husband,
    don't be a fool.
Working the night shift
    is ruining your tool.
It's better to go hungry
    the rest of your life
Than to bring home a pecker
    that's dead to your wife.
I have always been happy
    as your little queen.
But when at night you're
    nowhere to be seen,
And when you come home
    you can hardly creep,
I feel like screwing,
    but you want to sleep.

Each morning, dear husband,
    When you go to bed,
Your intention is good,
    but your pecker is dead.
I play with your pecker,
so wrinkled and dry.
I get so damn mad
    I could lay down and cry.

I have pleaded, dear husband,
    with tears in my eyes.
I played with your balls,
    but your pecker won't rise.
So I'll get a man
    who works through the day,
Then at night when you're gone,
    I'll get a good lay.
For in all the world
    there is only one sin
For which there is no pardon,
    or never has been.
For that is a man
    who is foolish and mean.
Who gives up his screwing
    to run a newsroom.

Ladies, Are You Getting All You're Supposed to Get?

Girls, did you know that the average lay requires thirty strokes of six inches each, or 180 inches?

An average girl can take three lays a week, that is, 540 inches or 45 feet of peter a week,

Which means she accepts 2,340 feet of peter a year.

Since a mile is 5,280 feet, we learn that girls get approximately half a mile of peter a year.

So girls, if you're not getting half a mile of peter a year, you're getting screwed and don't know it!

Why Beer Is Better
than Women

1. You can enjoy a beer all month long.
2. Beer stains wash out.
3. You don't have to wine and dine beer.
4. Your beer will always wait patiently for you in the car while you play hockey.
5. When your beer goes flat, you toss it.
6. Beer is never late.
7. Hangovers go away.
8. A beer doesn't get jealous when you grab another beer.
9. Beer labels come off without a fight.
10. When you go to a bar, you know you can always pick up a beer.
11. Beer never has a headache.
12. After you have had a beer, the bottle is still worth ten cents.
13. A beer won't get upset if you come home and have beer on your breath.
14. If you pour a beer right, you'll always get good head.
15. You can have more than one beer in a night and not feel guilty.
16. A beer always goes down easy.
17. You can share a beer with your friends.
18. You always know when you're the first one to pop a beer.
19. A beer is always wet.
20. Beer doesn't demand equality.
21. You can have a beer in public.
22. A beer doesn't care when you come.
23. A frigid beer is a good beer.
24. You don't have to wash a beer before it tastes good.

How You Can Tell When It's Going to Be a Rotten Day

You wake up facedown on the pavement.

You put your bra on backward, and it fits better.

You call suicide prevention, and they put you on hold.

You see a *60 Minutes* news team waiting in your office.

Your birthday cake collapses from the weight of the candles.

Your son tells you he wishes Anita Bryant would mind her own business.

You want to put on the clothes you wore home from the party, and there aren't any.

You turn on the news, and they're showing emergency routes out of the city.

Your twin sister forgot your birthday.

You wake up and discover your waterbed broke, and then realize that you don't have a waterbed.

Your car horn goes off accidentally and remains stuck as you follow a group of Hell's Angels on the freeway.

Your wife wakes up feeling amorous, and you have a headache.

Your boss tells you not to bother to take off your coat.

The bird singing outside your window is a buzzard.

You wake up, and your braces are locked together.

You walk to work and find your dress is stuck in the back of your pantyhose.

You call your answering service, and they tell you it's none of your business.

Your blind date turns out to be your ex-wife.

Your income tax check bounces.

You put both contact lenses in the same eye.

Your pet rock snaps at you.

Your wife says, "Good morning, Bill," and your name is George.

(Author unknown ... but troubled)

Sexcuse

If you ever wondered what might lead some husbands to drinking, sometimes to the point of becoming completely stoned, not to mention the rate at which they might seek the company of other women (cheat), perhaps the following will shed a little light on the matter:

To My Loving Wife:

During the past year, I have tried to seduce you 365 times. I have succeeded only thirty-six times. This is, on average, once every ten days. The following is a list of why I did not succeed more often:

1.	We'll wake the children.	17 times
2.	It's too late.	23 times
3.	It's too hot.	15 times
4.	It's too cold.	5 times
5.	It's too early.	15 times
6.	Pretending to be asleep	49 times
7.	Window are open, so the neighbors will hear.	9 times
8.	Backache	??? times
9.	Headache	4 times
10.	Toothache	6 times
11.	Gigglers	4 times
12.	Too full.	10 times
13.	Not in the mood.	21 times
14.	Baby is crying.	17 times
15.	Watched late TV show.	7 times
16.	I watched late TV show.	5 times
17.	Mudpack	3 times
18.	New hairdo	25 times
19.	There's company in next room.	11 times
20.	You had to go to bathroom.	19 times
	Total	329 times

During the thirty-six times I did succeed, the activity was not entirely satisfactory because:

Six times you chewed gum the whole time.
Five times you watched TV the whole time.
Eighteen times you told me to hurry up and get through with it.
Six times I had to wake you and tell you we were through.
One time I was afraid I had hurt you because I felt you move.

Honey, it's no damn wonder I drink too much!

Your loving husband

The Signifying Monkey

There's one in every neighborhood. You know the brother I mean. Generally shorter than the others. Uglier. The lamest cat on the block. And probably the only virgin.

This oddity's only claim to fame is that he's probably got the biggest mouth and the quickest feet. The blazing speed he shows has been the only thing that has kept him alive. He's a shit talker. One of those brothers who lay back and try to instigate something to generate some excitement or simply to show the world that he's the best man.

Old or young, he's the slickest and quickest inmate in the urban jungle and comes on a helluva lot stronger than his light-in-the-ass frame is prepared to back up. And he sometimes wins. Check him out:

Deep down in the jungle where the tall grass grew,
Lived the signifyingest monkey the world ever knew.
He was up in a tree, just snoring a bit,
When he thought he'd come up with some of his shit.
Now, down on the ground in a great big ring
Lived a bad-ass lion who knew he was king.
The signifying monkey spied the lion one day
And said, "I heard some???. You down?"

??? ther-
??? there,

"And the way he talks would curl your hair.
From what he said, he ain't your friend
'Cause he said your ass he'll surely bend.
This burly motherfucker says your mammy's a whore,
And your sister turns tricks on the cabin floor.
And he talked 'bout your wife in a hell of a way.
Said the whole jungle fucked her just the other day.
If he said that 'bout my bitch, he'd have to pay.
I'd whip his ass all motherfucking day."

TED CARELOCK

Now the lion jumped up full of rage,
Like a ditty bopper ready to rampage.
He ran through the jungle like death on a breeze,
Knocking all the coconuts off the trees.
He came on a hippo just lying around
And said, "Come on, motherfucker, let's get down."
Hippo said, "Don't come messin' wit' me.
The one you want is behind that tree."
He dug the elephant behind a pine
And said, "Come on, motherfucker, your ass is mine."
The elephant looked out from the corner of his eyes
And said, "Ain't you better pick on someone your size?"
Old lion jumped up with a mighty pass,
But elephant knocked him dead on his ass.
He romped and stomped and fucked up his face,
Kicked him so hard he knocked his ass out of place.
They fought all night and half the next day,
And I still don't know how the lion got away.
But back he came, more dead than alive,
And the monkey came up with more of his jive.
The monkey had been watching from his tree all the while
And started signifying in true monkey style.
He said, "Hey, Mr. Lion, you sure look sad.
That cocksucker must have really been bad.
When you left here you were yelling like a pup.
Now look at you—you're all fucked up.
Sheeeeeiit! That elephant sure gave you hell.
Why, he whipped your ass into a shitting spell.
You look like a whore with the seven-year itch.
'King of the jungle,' ain't you a bitch?
And don't tell me you didn't get beat.
'Cause my bitch and I had a ringside seat.
Every time I'm up here ripping off a bit,
Here you come with that rah-rah shit.
Now go on; get your ass out from under my tree
Before I swing out there and spray you with pee."

The monkey jumped up, down, and around
Till his foot missed a limb, and his ass hit the ground.
Lion took off with a helluva roar,
His tail popping like a Colt .44.
Like a bolt of lightning and a streak of heat,
The lion jumped the monkey with all four feet.
The monkey looked up with tears in his eyes
And said, "Goddamn, Mr. Lion, I apologize!"
Lion said, "No use your pleading and crying
'Cause I'm going to put an end to your signifying."
Monkey saw that he couldn't get away,
So he had to think of something to say.
Lion said, "Mr. Monkey, make your last request."
Monkey said, "Get your feet off my motherfucking chest.
I know you think you're raising hell
Just because you caught me when I slipped and fell.
But just let me get my ass off the ground and my balls out of the sand,
And I'll whip your ass like a natural man.
If you let me up like a fighting man should,
I'll kick your old ass all over these woods."
Now such a bold challenge the lion'd never had,
And it made the old lion fighting mad.
So he backed off, ready for a fight,
And the signifying monkey jumped clear out of sight.
Flying through the air like a fired-up bee,
The signifying monkey landed in the highest tree.
Saying, "Mr. Lion, Mr. Lion, don't you know?
That's the bullshit that made the green grass grow.
Mr. Lion, Mr. Lion, you thought you were king,
But I found out you weren't a goddamned thing.
Down on the ground you think you're so tough,
Bring your ass up here, and I'll really get rough.
And if you ever fuck with me again,
I'll go out and get my elephant friend."
Then the monkey laughed and swung away,
Singing, "I'll live to signify one more day!"

TED CARELOCK

The Prayer of a Realist

Lord, thou knowest I am growing older.

Keep me from becoming talkative and possessed with the idea that I must express myself on every subject.

Release me from the craving to straighten out everyone's affairs.

Keep me from the <u>recital of endless detail</u>. Give me wings to get to the point.

Seal my lips when I am inclined to tell of my aches and my pains. They are increasing with the years, and my love to speak of them grows sweeter as time goes by.

Teach me the glorious lesson that occasionally I may be wrong. Make me thoughtful but not nosey, helpful but not bossy. With my vast store of wisdom and experience, it does not seem a pity not to use it all. But thou knowest, Lord, that I want a few friends at the end.

The Nun and the Bus Driver

A nun gets on a bus and sits behind the driver. She says to the bus driver that she needs someone to talk to. She lives in a convent and wants to experience sex before she dies. The bus driver agrees, but the nun explains she can't have sex with anyone who is married because it would be a sin. The bus driver says no problem, he's not married. The nun says she also has to die a virgin, so she'll have to take it in the ass. The bus driver agrees again, and being the only people on the bus, they go back in the back and take care of business.

When finished and he resumes driving, the bus driver says, "Sister, I have a confession to make. I'm married and have three kids."

The nun replies, "That's OK. I have a confession too. My name is Bruce, and I'm on my way to a costume party."

Subject: Marriage

A lawyer got married to a woman who had previously been married twelve times. On their wedding night, they settled into the bridal suite at their hotel, and the bride said to her new groom, "Please promise to be gentle. I am still a virgin."

This puzzled the groom since after twelve marriages, he thought that at least one of her husbands would have been able to perform. He asked his new bride to explain the phenomenon.

She responded, "My first husband was a sales representative who spent our entire marriage telling me, in grandiose terms, 'It's gonna be great!'

"My second husband was from software services. He was never quite sure how it was supposed to function, but he said he would send me documentation.

"My third husband was from field services and constantly said that everything was diagnostically OK, but he just couldn't get the system up.

"My fourth husband was from educational services, and he simply said, 'Those who can, do; those who can't, teach.'

"My fifth husband was from the telemarketing department and said that he had the orders, but he wasn't quite sure when he was going to be able to deliver.

"My sixth husband was an engineer. He told me that he understood the basic process but needed three years to research, implement, and design a new state-of-the-art method.

"My seventh husband was from finance and administration. His comments were that he knew how, but he just wasn't sure whether it was his job.

"My eighth husband was from standards and regulations and told me that he was up to the standards but that regulations said nothing about how to do it.

"My ninth husband was a marketing manager. He said, 'I know I have the product. I'm just not sure how to position it.'

"My tenth husband was a psychiatrist, and all he ever wanted to do was talk about it.

"My eleventh husband was a gynecologist, and all he ever wanted to do was look at it.

"My twelfth husband was a stamp collector, and all he ever wanted to do was … God, I miss him! So now I have married a lawyer, so I know I'm going to get screwed!"

Trojan Condom Company
6959 Slippery Root Drive
Droptrouser NC 22269

Dear

We regret to inform you that we have rejected your recent application to model and represent our product, Trojan Condoms.

Although your general appearance is not displeasing, our board of directors feels that your wearing of our product does not portray a positive, romantic image for our product. A loose, baggy, and wrinkled condom is not considered romantic.

We did admire your effort to firm it up by using Poly-Grip, but even then, it slipped off before we could get the photograph taken. We would like to note, however, that we have never seen a penis that looked like a bicycle grip until now.

We appreciate your interest and thank you for your time.
We will retain your application for future consideration, if by chance we decide that there is a market for Micro-Mini Condoms.

We send greetings and deepest sympathy to your wife and/or girlfriend.

Yours Very Truly,

Burly Dick, President
Trojan Condom Company

Pa/pee

PS: Remember our slogans:

> Cover your stump before you hump.
> Don't be silly, protect your willy.
> Before you attack her, wrap your whacker.
> If you're not going to sack it, go home and whack it!

A Surprise Gift for Wife

A wife whose husband only got excuses when he wanted to have sex was very happy when one day he came home with a box beautifully wrapped. To her surprise, she found six little cats. "Oh, how thoughtful," was her response.

"You think so?" asked the husband. "These cats will be pallbearers for your dead pussy!"

Name	Official Polish Sex Quiz	Score	
		True	False
1. A clitoris is a type of flower.			
2. A pubic hair is a wild rabbit.			
3. A vulva is a Swedish automobile.			
4. Spread eagle is an extinct bird.			
5. A Fallopian tube is part of a TV.			
6. It is dangerous to have a wet dream while sleeping with an electric blanket.			
7. "Vagina" is a medical term used to describe heart trouble.			
8. Fellatio is an Italian dagger.			
9. A menstrual cycle has three wheels.			
10. A G-string is part of a violin.			
11. "Semen" is another word for sailors.			
12. Anus is the Latin word for yearly.			
13. Testicles are found on an octopus.			
14. Cunnilingus is a person who speaks four languages.			
15. Asphalt describes rectal trouble.			
16. Kotex is a radio station in Texas.			
17. Masturbate is used to catch large fish.			
18. Coitus is a musical instrument.			
19. Fetus is a character on *Gunsmoke*.			
20. An umbilical cord is part of a parachute.			
21. A condom is an apartment complex.			
22. When you miss a period, you can use a semi-colon.			
23. Genitalia is the national airline of Italy.			
24. A dry hump is a dehydrated camel.			

Birth of a Candy Bar

One Payday, Mr. Goodbar wanted a Bit O' Honey, so he took Miss Hershey Behind the Power House on the corner of Clark and 5th Avenue. He began to feel her Mounds, and that was pure Almond Joy, which made his Tootsie Roll. Then he let out a Snicker, and his Butterfinger went up her Kit Kat and caused a Milky Way. She screamed, "O'Henry," as she squeezed his Peter Paul and his Zagnuts. Miss Hershey said, "You are better than three Musketeers." Soon she became a bit Chunky, and nine months later, she had a Baby Ruth.

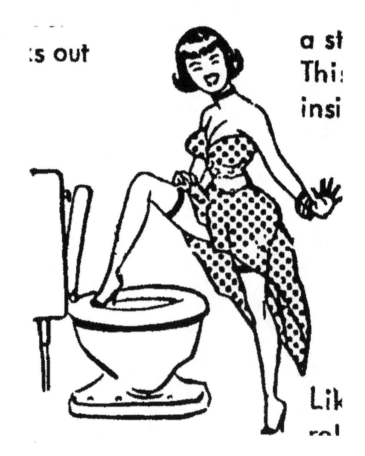

District Director

To: All Male Taxpayers

From: Internal Revenue Service

Subject: Increased Tax Payments

Dear Taxpayer:

The only thing the Internal Revenue Service has not taxed is your pecker. This is due to the fact that 40 percent of the time, it is hanging around unemployed; 30 percent of the time, it is pissed off; 20 percent of the time, it is hard up; and 10 percent of the time, it is employed but operates in the hole. Furthermore, it has two dependents, and they are both nuts.

Accordingly, after January 1985, your pecker will be taxed based on its size using the Pecker-Checker Scale shown below. Determine your category, and insert the additional tax under "Other Taxes," page 2, part V, ;ine 61 of your standard income tax return (Form 1040).

Pecker-Checker Scale

10–12	inches	Luxury Tax	$50.00
8–10	inches	Pole Tax	25.00
6–8	inches	Privilege Tax	15.00
4–6	inches	Nuisance Tax	5.00

Anyone under four (4) inches is eligible for a refund.**

Very truly yours,

Nancy J. Cutchapeckeroff
IRS Director, XVIII

**Do not apply for an extension.

Dear Son,

I'm writing this slow 'cause I know you can't read fast. We don't live where we did when you left. Your dad read in the paper where most accidents happened within twenty miles of home, so we moved. I won't be able to send you the address as the last Kentucky family who lived here took the numbers with them for their next house, so they wouldn't have to change their address.

This place has a washing machine. The first day I put four shirts in it, pulled the chain, and haven't seen 'em since. It only rained twice this week—three days the first time and four days the second time.

The coat you want me to send you, your aunt Sue said it would be a little too heavy to send in the mail with them heavy buttons, so we cut them off and put them in the pockets.

We got a bill from the funeral home. Said that if we didn't make the last payment on Grandma's funeral bill, up she comes.

About your father … he has a lovely new job. He has over five hundred men under him. He is cutting grass at the cemetery.

About your sister, she had a baby this morning, I haven't found out whether it is a boy or a girl, so I don't know if you are an aunt or uncle.

Your uncle John fell in the whiskey vat. Some man tried to pull him out, but he fought them off playfully, so he drowned. We cremated him. He burned for three days. Three of your friends went off the bridge in a pickup. One was driving; the other two were in the back. The driver got out. He rolled down the window and swam to safety. The other two drowned. They couldn't get the tailgate down.

Not much more news this time. Nothing much has happened.

Love,

Mom

PS. I was going to send you money, but the envelope was already sealed.

TED CARELOCK

My shovel! After I told him I had already broken six shovels shoveling all the shit he pushed into the driveway, I broke my last one over his fucking head.

Jan. 4: Finally got out the house today. Went to the store to get food, and on the way back, a damned deer ran in front of the car and hit it. Did about $3,000 damage to the car. Those fucking beasts should be killed. Wish the hunters had killed them all last November. Took the car to the garage in town. Would you believe the thing is rusting out from all that fucking salt they put on the roads?

May 10: Moved to Florida. I can't imagine why anyone in their right mind would ever live in the godforsaken state of New York!

To My "White" Friends

For the white person who wants to know how to be my friend,
The first thing you do is to forget that I'm black.
Second, you must never forget that I'm black.

You should be able to dig Aretha,
But don't play her every time I come over.
And if you decide to play Beethoven, don't tell me
His life story; they made us take music too.

Eat soul food if you like, but don't expect me
To locate your restaurants
Or cook it for you.

And if some Black person insults you,
Mugs you, rapes your sister, rapes you,
Rips your house, or is just being an ass,
Please, do not apologize to me
For wanting to do them bodily harm.
It make me wonder if you're foolish.

In other words, if you really want to be my friend, don't make a labor of
it. I'm lazy, remember?

Subject: FW: No Panties

There were three old black ladies getting ready to take a plane trip for the first time. The first lady said, "I don't know 'bout y'all, but I'm gunna wear me some hot=pink panties beefo' I gets on dat plane."

"Why you gonna wear dem fo'?" the other two asked.

The first replied, "'Cause if dat plane goes down, and I'm out dare laying butt-up in a conefield, dey gonna find me first."

The second lady said, "Well, I'm a-gonna wear me some fluorescent-orange panties."

"Why you gonna wear dem?" the others asked.

The second lady answered, "'Cause if dis hare plane is goin' down, and I be floating butt-up in the ocean, dey can see me first."

The third old lady said, "Well, I'm not going to wear any panties."

"What? No panties?" the others asked in disbelief.

The third lady replied, "Dat's right, girlfriends, you hears me right. I ain't wearin' any panties 'cause if dis plane goes down, honey, dey always look fo da black box first."

A Dick

I've got a head I can't think with.
An eye I can't see out of.
I have to hang around with two nuts all the time.
My closest neighbor is an asshole.
Worst of all, my owner beats me all the time.
And my best friend is a pussy!
And now, because of AIDS, I have to wear this rubber suit and throw up all over myself!
It ain't easy being a dick!

TED CARELOCK

Crotch Master 6000

The Snake That Poisons Everybody

It
topples
governments;
wrecks
marriages;
ruins
careers;
busts
reputations;
causes
heartaches,
nightmares,
indigestion;
spawns suspicion;
generates
grief;
dispatches
innocent
people
to cry in their
pillows.
Even its name
hisses.
It's called
gossip.
Office gossip,
shop gossip,
party gossip.

It makes
headlines
and headaches.
Before
you repeat
a story,
ask yourself:
Is it true?
Is it fair?
Is it necessary?
If not,
shut up.

Gotta Pee

Two women friends had gone for a girls' night out.

Both were very faithful and loving wives. However, they got overenthusiastic on the Bacardi Breezers. Incredibly drunk, while walking home, they needed to pee. So they stopped in the cemetery.

Neither had anything to wipe with, so one of them decided to take off her panties and use them.

Her friend, however, was wearing a rather expensive pair of panties and did not want to ruin them. She was lucky enough to squat next to a grave that had a wreath with a ribbon on it. So she proceeded to wipe with that.

After the girls did their business, they continued on home.

The next day, one of the women's husband was concerned that his normally sweet and innocent wife was still in bed, hungover. So he phoned the other husband and said, "These girls' nights out have got to stop! I'm starting to suspect the worst. My wife came home with no panties!"

"That's nothing," said the other husband. "Mine came back with a card stuck to her butt that said, 'From all of us at the fire station. We'll never forget you.'"

TED CARELOCK

Biker with Problems

A short guy is sitting at a bar just staring at his drink for half an hour when this big, trouble-making biker comes up next to him, grabs his drink, and gulps it down in one swig. Then he turns to the guy with a menacing stare as if to say, "What'cha gonna do about it?"

The poor little guy starts crying.

"Come on, man. I was just giving you a hard time," the biker says. "I didn't think you'd cry. I can't stand to see a man crying."

"This is the worst day of my life," says the little guy between sobs. "I can't do anything right. I overslept and was late to an important meeting, so my boss fired me. When I went to the parking lot and found my car was stolen, and I don't have any insurance. I left my wallet in the cab I took home," he continues, crying even harder. "Then I found my wife in bed with the gardener, and my dog bit me. So I came to this bar, trying to work up the courage to put an end to my life. And then you show up and drink the damn poison."

Edible Complex

A while back, some lawyers and writers from Minneapolis sent us a manuscript that will become *The Cucumber Book* (due out this spring from M. Evans). The book discusses why cucumbers are better than men. The idea, if not the manuscript, made the underground rounds, and in retaliation, taco jokes soon sprang up. Before the third category hits (we hear that broccoli jokes aimed at the sexually unevolved are next), we thought we'd bring you up to date with the phenomenon.

Cucumbers are better than men because:

Cucumbers don't make you cry.

Cucumbers taste better.

A cucumber will never give you a hickey.

A cucumber isn't allergic to your cat.

A cucumber doesn't use your toothbrush.

A cucumber will never leave you (A) for another woman, (B) for another man, (C) for another cucumber.

You always know where your cucumber has been.

Cucumbers can get away any weekend.

Cucumbers can always wait until you get home.

Cucumbers aren't into rope and leather, talking dirty, or swinging with fruits and nuts.

You can have as many cucumbers as you can handle.

You have to eat cucumbers only when you feel like it.

Cucumbers never answer your phone or borrow your car.

Cucumbers won't go through your medicine chest.

Cucumbers never make a scene because there are other cucumbers in the refrigerator.

No matter how old you are, you can always get a fresh cucumber.

Cucumbers don't leave whisker burns, fall asleep on your chest, or drool on the pillow.

Cucumbers don't expect to be put through law school.

A cucumber won't tell you it's outgrown you intellectually.

It's easy to drop a cucumber.

Tacos are better than women because:
Tacos won't shave with your razor.
Tacos won't ask, "Is there another taco?"
Tacos won't look through your checkbook.
Tacos don't have cats.
A taco won't mind if you share it with a friend.
A taco never asks, (A) "Is it hard yet?" (B) "Is it in yet?" (C) "Have
     you seen a doctor about that?"
A taco won't tell other tacos about your cucumber.
Tacos are ready when you are.
Tacos never ask you to call them in the morning.
With a taco, you never have to say you're sorry.
You don't have to respect tacos in the morning.
You don't have to tell tacos you love them.
Tacos don't fall in love with you just because you have sex.
Tacos don't make you wear a condom.
Tacos are happy to sleep on the wet spot.
Tacos don't get upset if you eat other tacos.
You don't have to hold a taco while it's falling asleep.
Tacos never have headaches.
Tacos don't leave hair in your teeth.
Tacos don't care if you're married.
Tacos never even talk about marriage.
Tacos don't get pregnant.
Tacos don't insist on foreplay.
Tacos don't bite.
You can have your taco as hot as you want it.

How Many Dirty Words
Do You Know?

Can you find sixty-seven sex words and terms?

These words are hidden in the block frontwards, backwards, up, down, and diagonally. Go for it!

ABORTION	FONDLE	PENIS
ANAL	FRENCH	PISS
ASS	FUCK	PRICK
BASTARD	GOOSE	PUSSY
BEAT	HARD	SALIVA
BED	HEAD	SCREW
BITCH	HEAT	SHIT
BREAST	HELL	SIN
BUGGER	HOLE	SLUT
BUST	HOTS	SMEGMA
CLIT	IUD	SODOMIZE
COCK	JERK-OFF	SON-OF-A-BITCH
COME	JISM	SPERM
CROTCH	KISS	SUCK
CUNT	LABIA	SWAP
DAMN	LIPS	TITS
DICK	MASTURBATION	TONGUE
DILDO	MEAT	TOUCH
DINGLEBERRY	MOAN	TWAT
EAT	MOTHERFUCKER	VAGINA
FART	NIPPLE	VD
FEEL	NUTS	
FINGER	PEE	

Do Not Open Page until You Have Decided Which Person You Are

1. The vain person
2. The amiable person
3. The proud person
4. The shy person
5. The impudent person
6. The scientific person
7. The unfortunate person
8. The nervous person
9. The dishonest person
10. The honest person
11. The foolish person.
12. The thrifty person
13. The antisocial person
14. The strategic person
15. The sadistic person
16. The intellectual person
17. The athletic person
18. The miserable person
19. The sensitive person

1. One who loves the smell of his own farts.
2. One who loves the smell of other people's farts.
3. One who thinks his farts are exceptionally fine.
4. One who releases silent farts and then blushes.
5. One who boldly farts out loud and then laughs.
6. One who farts regularly but is truly concerned about pollution.
7. One who tries awfully hard to fart but shits instead.
8. One who stops in the middle of a fart.
9. One who farts and then blames the dog.

10. One who admits he farted but offers a good medical reason.
11. One who suppresses a fart for hours and hours.
12. One who always has several good farts in reserve.
13. One who excuses himself and farts in complete privacy.
14. One who conceals his farts with loud laughing.
15. One who farts in bed and then fluffs the bedcover over his head.
16. One who can determine from the smell of his neighbor's fart the latest food items consumed.
17. One who farts at the slightest exertion.
18. One who would truly love to but can't fart at all.
19. One who farts and then starts crying.

"I Am Going to Be Builder When I Grow Up"

Did you hear about little Jimmy? He is four years old. He was bugging his mother, so she said, "Jimmy, why don't you go across the street and watch the builders work. Maybe you'll learn something."

Jimmy was gone for about two hours. When he came home, his mother asked him what he had learned.

Jimmy replied, "Well, first you put the goddamn door up. Then the son of a bitch doesn't fit. So you have to take the cocksucker back down. Then you have to trim a cunt hair off each side and put the motherfucker back up.

Shocked, Jimmy's mother said, "You wait till your father gets home."

When Jimmy's dad got home, Mom told him to ask Jimmy what he learned across the street. Jimmy told the whole story.

After listening to his son's story, he said, "Jimmy, you go outside and get me a switch."

Jimmy replied," Fuck you. That's the electrician's job."

How to Know You Are Growing Older

Everything hurts, and what doesn't hurt, doesn't work.

The gleam in your eye is from the sun hitting your bifocals.

You feel like the night before, and you haven't been anywhere.

Your little black book contains only names ending in in MD.

You get winded playing cards.

Your children begin to look middle-aged.

You join a health club and don't go.

A dripping faucet causes an uncontrollable bladder urge.

You look forward to dull evenings.

You know all the answers, but nobody asks you the questions.

You need glasses to find your glasses.

You turn out the lights for economic rather than romantic reasons.

You sit in a rocking chair and can't get it going.

Your knees buckle, but your belt won't.

Your back goes out more than you do.

You have too much room in the house and not enough in the medicine chest.

You sink your teeth in steak, and they stay there.

You wonder why more people aren't using this size print!

Golden Years

The golden years are here at last.

I cannot see; I cannot pee.

I cannot chew; I cannot screw.

My memory shrinks; my hearing shrinks.

No sense of smell; I look like hell.

The golden years have come at last.

The golden years can kiss my ass.

Dumb Men Jokes: Strange but True

Why are all dumb blonde jokes one-liners?
>So men can understand them.

What is the difference between government bonds and men?
>Government bonds mature.

What's a man's idea of helping with the housework?
>Lifting his legs so you can vacuum.

What's the difference between a man and ET?
>ET phoned home.

Why is psychoanalysis a lot quicker for men than for women?
>When it's time to go back to his childhood, he's already there.

What did God say after He created man?
>"I can do better than this."

How do men define a 50–50 relationship?
>They cook/we eat; they clean/we dirty; they iron/we wrinkle.

What's the best way to force a man to do sit-ups?
>Put the remote control between his toes.

How do men exercise at the beach?
>By sucking in their stomachs every time they see a bikini.

What does a man consider to be a seven-course meal?
>A hot dog and a six-pack.

How are men like noodles?
>They are always in hot water, they lack taste, and they need dough.

Why is it good that there are female astronauts?
>When the crew gets lost in space, at least the women will ask for directions.

The 747 Has Everything

A man traveling by plane was in urgent need of using the men's room. Each time he tried the door, it was occupied. The stewardess, aware of his predicament, suggested that he use the ladies' room but cautioned him against pressing any of the buttons on the wall. The buttons were marked WW, WA, PP, and ATR. But eventually, his curiosity got the better of him, and sitting there, he carefully pressed the first button, WW. Immediately, warm water sprayed gently over his entire ass. He thought, *Golly, the gals really have it made.*

Still curious, he pressed the WA button. Warm air dried his ass completely. *This,* he thought, *is out of this world.* The button marked PP yielded a large powder puff, which patted his bottom lightly with a scented powder. Naturally, he just couldn't resist the last button, the one marked ATR.

When he awoke in the hospital, he panicked and buzzed for the nurse. When she appeared, he cried out, "What happened? The last thing I remember, I was in the ladies' room aboard a plane."

The nurse replied, "Yes, you were. But you were cautioned about pressing the buttons. You were really having a great time until you pressed the button marked ATR, which stands for automatic Tampax remover. Your penis is under your pillow."

Teenagers!

Tired of being
hassled
by your
stupid parents?
Act now!

Move out, get a job,
pay your own bills
while you still know everything!

True Happiness Is Like the Butterfly

The more you pursue it, the more it will elude you.
But if you are patient and still, it will come softly and land on your shoulder.

The Creation of a Pussy

Seven wise men with knowledge so fine
    created a pussy to their design.
First was a butcher, smart with wit,
    using a knife, he gave it a slit.
Second was a carpenter, strong and bold,
    with a hammer and chisel, he gave it a hole.
Third was a tailor, tall and thin,
    by using red velvet, he lined it within.
Fourth was a hunter, short and stout,
    with a piece of fox fur, he lined it without.
Fifth was a fisherman, nasty as hell,
    threw in a fish and gave it a smell.
Sixth was a preacher whose name was McGee,
    touched it and blessed it and said it could pee.
Last came a sailor, dirty little runt,
    he sucked it and fucked it and called it a cunt.

You Put the Devil Out, but You Let Him Leave His Bags

This is powerful!

You got out of a relationship because it was bad,
but you are still resentful and angry.
You let the devil leave his bags.

You got out of financial debt, but you still can't
control your desire to spend on frivolous things.
You let the devil leave his bags.

You got out of a bad habit or addiction, but you still long
to
try it just one more time.
You let the devil leave his bags.

You said, "I forgive you," but you can't seem to forget and
have
peace with that person.
You let the devil leave his bags.

You told your unequally yoked mate that it was over,
but you continue to call.
You let the devil leave his bags.

You got out of that horribly oppressive job, but you are
still
trying to sabotage the company after you've left.
You let the devil leave his bags.

You cut off the affair with that married man/woman, but you
still lust after him/her.
You let the devil leave his bags.

You broke off your relationship with that hurtful, abusive
person, but you are
suspicious and distrusting of every new person you
meet.
You let the devil leave his bags.

You let go of the past hurts from growing up
in an
unstable environment, yet you believe you are unworthy
of love from anyone.
You let the devil leave his bags.

When you put the devil out,
please make sure he takes his
bags, or
he is never really gone.
You know,
sometimes, we go all out to
the point of losing sleep,
trying to hold on to the same
old, filthy mess God is trying
to rid us of, so he can replace
it with something good!
In 2009, let the devil
take his bags with him!
Be blessed, healthy, and
happy.

Trials keep you strong,
and sorrows keep you human.
Failures keep you humble.
Success keeps you glowing.
But only God keeps you going!

TED CARELOCK

Lady in Tiffany

A lady walks into Tiffany. She looks around, spots a beautiful diamond bracelet, and walks over to inspect it.

As she bends over to look more closely, she unexpectedly farts. Very embarrassed, she looks around nervously to see if anyone noticed her little woops and prays that a salesperson was not anywhere near.

As she turns around, her worst nightmare materializes in the form of a salesman standing right behind her. Good-looking as well. Cool as a cucumber, he displays all of the qualities one would expect of a professional in a store like Tiffany.

He politely greets the lady with, "Good day, madam. How may we help you today?"

Blushing and uncomfortable, but still hoping that the salesman somehow missed her little "incident," she asks, "Sir, what is the price of this lovely bracelet?"

He answers, "Madam, if you farted just looking at it, you're going to shit when I tell you the price."

Bank Robber

A man with a gun went into a bank and demanded their money. Once he given the money, he turned to a customer and asked, "Did you see me rob this bank?"

The man replied, "Yes sir, I did." The robber then shot him in the temple, killing him instantly. He then turned to a couple standing next and asked the man, "Did you see me rob this bank?"

The man replied, "No sir, I didn't. But my wife did."

You Know You're a New Yorker

1. You say, "the city," and expect everyone to know that this means Manhattan.

2. You have never been to the Statue of Liberty or the Empire State Building.

3. You can get into a four-hour argument about how to get from Columbus Circle to Battery Park at 3:30 on the Friday before a long weekend but can't find Wisconsin on a map.

4. Hookers and the homeless are invisible.

5. You have a minimum of five worst cab ride ever stories.

6. You don't notice sirens anymore.

7. You live in a building with a population larger than most American towns.

8. Your doorman is Russian, your grocer is Korean, your deli man is Israeli, your building super is Italian, your laundry guy is Chinese, your favorite bartender is Irish, your favorite diner owner is Greek, the watch seller on your corner is Senegalese, your last cabbie was Pakistani, your newsstand guy is Indian, and your favorite falafel guy is Egyptian.

9. You're suspicious of strangers who are actually nice to you.

10. You secretly envy cabbies for their driving skills.

11. You think $7.00 to cross a bridge is a fair price.

12. Your door has more than three locks.

13. Your favorite movie has DeNiro in it.

14. You consider eye contact an act of overt aggression.

15. You run when you see a flashing "Do Not Walk" sign at the intersection.

16. You're thirty-five years old and don't have a driver's license.

17. You ride in a subway car with no air-conditioning just because there are seats available.

18. You're willing to take in strange people as roommates simply to help pay the rent.

19. There is no north or south; it's uptown or downtown.

20. When you're away from home, you miss "real" pizza and "real" bagels.

21. You know the differences between all the Ray's Pizzas.

22. You're not in the least bit interested in going to Times Square on New Year's Eve.

23. Your internal clock is permanently set to know when alternate side of the street parking regulations are in effect.

24. You know what a bodega is.

25. You know how to fold the *New York Times* in half vertically so that you can read it on the subway or bus without knocking off other passengers' hats.

26. Someone bumps into you, and you check for your wallet.

Are You a Real New Yorker?

You believe that being able to swear at people in their own language makes you multilingual.

You've considered stabbing someone just for saying, "the Big Apple."

The most frequently used part of your car is the horn.

You call an eight-foot by ten-foot plot of patchy grass a yard.

You consider Westchester "upstate."

You think Central Park is nature.

You're paying $1,200 for a studio apartment the size of a walk-in closet and think it is a real steal.

You've been to New Jersey twice and were hopelessly lost both times.

You pay more each month to park your car than most people in the United States pay in rent.

You go to dinner at 9 o'clock and then head out to the club when most Americans are heading to bed. You pay $5 for a beer without blinking that cost the bar 28 cents.

You take fashion seriously, but your closet is filled with mostly black clothes.

You have twenty-seven different menus next to your phone.

You consider going to Brooklyn a road trip.

You've gotten jaywalking down to an art form.

You take a taxi to get to your health club to exercise.

Fifty dollars' worth of groceries fits in one grocery bag.

A film crew on your block doesn't excite you but annoys the hell out of you.

People from other states can tell you are from New York from the second you open your mouth.

New York's local news is national.

You walk a mile in twelve minutes and think everything should be open 24/7 for you.

Are You a True New Yorker

A yellow light means speed up.

Red traffic means speed up because you know you have a one-second pause until the other turns green.

When communicating with other drivers on the road, it takes only one finger.

You order your dinner and have it delivered from the place across the street.

You cross the street on a green light, and if you get hit by a car, you blame the driver for not watching where he was going.

You can tell a gunshot from a firecracker and not get scared, but when you go to the burbs, you get scared of hearing a cricket.

You know the lights above the skyscrapers are the closest things we have to stars.

Blonde Phone Call

Hi, Mom. How are?

"Hi, Sally. Where you? I thought you were with your father at Ace Hardware."

"Yeah, we were, but I got arrested, and they've let me make one phone call."

"What happened?"

"Oh, I punched this African American woman in the head."

"What on earth? Why did you do that?"

"Well, it wasn't my fault. Dad told me to go find a Black & Decker."

*   *   *

If a woman with big boobs can work at Hooters, where can a one-legged woman work? IHOP.

Serenity

Lord, grant me the serenity to accept the things I cannot change, the courage to change the things I can, and the wisdom to hide the bodies of those people I had to kill because they pissed me off.

New Job at Walmart

So after landing my new job as a Walmart greeter,
a good find for many retirees,
I lasted less than a day.
About two hours into my first day on the job, a very loud,
unattractive, mean-acting woman walked
into the store with her two kids,
yelling obscenities at them all the way through the entrance.
As I had been instructed, I said pleasantly,
"Good morning, and welcome to
Walmart.
Nice children you have there. Are they twins?"
The ugly woman stopped yelling long enough to say,
"Hell no, they ain't twins. The oldest one's
nine, and the other one's seven.
Why the hell would you think they're twins?
Are you blind or just stupid?"
So I replied,
"I'm neither blind nor stupid, ma'am.
I just couldn't believe someone slept with you twice.
Have a good day, and thank you for shopping at Walmart."
My supervisor said I probably wasn't cut out for this line of work.

FUNNY
OFFICE
MEMOS

Notice: ☞ While in here, speak in a low, soothing tone, and do *not* disagree with me in any manner.

Please be informed that when one has reached "my age," noise and nonconcurrence cause gastric hyperperistalisis, hypersecretion of hydrochloric acid, and rubus of the gastric mucosa. And I become most unpleasant!

Sick of Working Forty Hours or More Each Week Just to Feed Your Family?

Would You Like to Relax All Day and Still Have All the Benefits of a Full-Time Bob?

If you answered yes to any of these questions, then you should consider moving to New York, "the Welfare State." If you qualify—and only working people do not—

you can receive the following:

> *Free* Housing
> *Free* Utilities
> *Free* Food
> *Free* Medical Insurance (with no limits or deductibles)
> *Free* Cash (for cigarettes, beer, drugs, etc.)
>> *Free* Transportation
>> *Free* Legal Services

This program is *not* limited to three to six months like in other states. In New York, you can collect *for life*. Some of our families have received benefits for two or three generations.

So if you would like to receive all this *without* working for a living, just call the New York State Department of Social Services.

PS: New York does not have a residency requirement, so you can, from another state—or country—today!

Paid Advertisement

Let's Get Rid of "the Girl"

Wouldn't 1979 be
a great year
to take one giant
step forward
for womankind
and get rid of
"the girl"?
Your attorney says,
"If I'm not here,
just leave it with
the girl."
The purchasing agent
says, "Drop off your
bid with the girl."
A manager says,
"My girl will get
back to your girl."
What girl?
Do they mean
Miss Rose?
Do they mean
Ms. Torres?
Do they mean
Mrs. McCullough?
Do they mean
Joy Jackson?
"The girl"
is certainly
a woman when she's
out of her teens.
Like you,
she has a name.
Use it.

TED CARELOCK

God, I Love This Place

Please be patient.
I only work here because
I am too old for a paper route,
too young for Social Security,
and too tired to have an affair.

Rules of This Office

1. This place has been designated as an "off-ice." Here, our employees may relax from the strenuous activities of home life.

2. Head of business shall be referred to as em-ploy-er, not fathead, old gumshoe, old pinchgut, or other usual terms.

3. In case of death, lie down. Name can then be dropped from payroll, and committee will be appointed to collect fund for flowers and conduct lottery for deceased's former job.

4. Secretaries and file clerks must be given a handicap of a desk length before being chased through the office. (At their own request, this rule shall not apply to female employees over thirty-five.)

5. In case of fire:
   a. Awaken your sleeping fellow employees slowly to prevent nervous shock.
   b. Leave by the new steel stairway that management will erect immediately after this fire.
   c. Leave like you do at 5 p.m.

6. Employees should feel free to make suggestions. Suggestions cost nothing. (And frankly, the ones that have been received lately are worth even less.)

7. Starting January 1, a new policy known as work breaks will be inaugurated. It is hoped that employees will try and fit this in to their already busy schedules of coffee breaks, lunch hours, rest periods, vacations, and days off.

TED CARELOCK

To: **Head of Personnel, Executive Office, New York**
Subject: **New Sick Leave Policy**

It has been brought to our attention that the attendance record of this organization is a disgrace to our gracious benefactors, who at your own request, gave you your job. Due to your lack of consideration for your jobs with so fine a concern, as shown by such frequent absenteeism, it has become necessary for us to revise some of our policies. The following changes become effective as of the above date:

Sickness: No excuse. We will no longer accept your doctor's statement as proof as we believe that if you are able to go to the doctor, you are able to come to work.

Death
(other than your own):   No excuse. There is nothing you can do for them, and we are sure that someone else with a lesser position can attend to the arrangement. However, if the funeral can be held in the late afternoon, we will be glad to let you off one hour early, provided that your share of the work is ahead enough to keep the job going in your absence.

Leave of Absence
(for an operation):   We are no longer allowing this practice. We wish to discourage any thoughts that you may need an operation as we believe that as long as you are an employee here, you will need all of whatever you have and should not consider having anything removed. We hired you as you are, and to have anything removed would certainly make you less than what we bargained for.

Death (your own):   This will be accepted as an excuse, but we would like a two-week notice as we feel it is your duty to train someone else for your job.

Also, entirely too much time is being spent in the restroom. In the future, we will follow the practice of going in alphabetical order. For instance, those whose names begin with A will go from 8:00 to 8:10, B will go from 8:15 to 8:30, and so on. If you are unable to go at your time, it will be necessary to wait until the day when your turn comes again.

AB: cd

Company Rules

(Must Be Memorized)

Rule 1:   The boss is *always* right.

Rule 2:   In the impossible hypothesis that a subordinate may be right, Rule 1 becomes immediately operative.

Rule 3:   The boss does not sleep; he rests.

Rule 4:   The boss is never late; he is delayed elsewhere.

Rule 5:   The boss never leaves his work; his presence is required elsewhere.

Rule 6:   The boss never reads the paper in his office; he studies.

Rule 7:   The boss never takes liberties with his secretary; he educates her.

Rule 8:   Whoever enters the boss's office with an idea of his or her own must leave that office with the boss's ideas.

Rule 9:   The boss is always boss, even in bathing togs.

Rule 10:   The boss is *always* right.

Interoffice Memo No. 69

Management wishes to bring to the attention of all personnel the fact that some individuals have been using abusive language in the exchange of normal verbal communication with relation to the performance of routine activities on the premises. This practice must cease immediately.

The following coded list is provided to permit individual freedom of expression and allow all to express frustrations in a clear, concise manner. It will prove a very effective tool, and if employed properly, will offend no one with delicate ears.

To prevent mistaking these communications codes with department numbers and/or telephone extensions, management has assigned the 800 and 900 series numbers to be utilized for your convenience and clarity.

801	You gotta be shitting me.
802	Get off my fucking back.
803	Beats the shit out of me.
804	What the fuck?
805	It's so fucking bad I can't believe it.
806	I hate this fucking place.
807	This place sucks.
808	Fuck you very much!
809	Lovely, simply fucking lovely!
810	That darn club.
811	Fuck, shit, piss!
812	Get beat!
813	Kiss my ass, buddy.
814	I really don't give a shit.
815	Fuck it, I'm on salary.
816	Stick it in your fucking ear!
817	Piss on the whole fucking project.

818	Fuck it, just plain fuck it.
819	Hot shit!
820	Hot, fucking shit.
821	Bitchin'.
822	Tell someone who gives a shit.
823	Don't get so fucking wise, guy.
824	I don't give a fuck. So there.
825	Fuck you in the heart, Jack.
826	You son of a bitch.
827	Whatever you say, asshole.
828	Who the fuck was that?
828	What the fuck was that?
829	Fuck you!
830	Fuck you _too_!
831	It won't fucking work!
832	Go pound sand in your ass.
833	Fuck off!
834	Who called this fucking meeting?
835	Fucked up beyond repair.
836	Adiós, motherfucker!
837	Idiot, you don't know your ass from first base!
838	Fuck you too.
839	No shit.
840	No fucking shit.
841	Go to hell, asshole.
842	Stick it in your fucking ear!
900	Unbefuckingly believable!
901	Cool it. This is my wife/husband; follow my lead.
902	I'm free this weekend.
903	Take your time; I don't want to be stuck with this ass for lunch.
904	Help me unload this mother.
905	Hey, baby, let's ball at lunch.
906	I'm free tonight.

907	Tied up with my wife/husband tonight.
908	My wife/husband is out of town.
910	Let's take off sick together.
911	Meet you at the motel.
912	Let's trade balling partners.
913	Sorry, darling, but it's that time.
914	Will she or won't she?
915	Will he or won't he?
916	B.O.B. (buzz off, bitch).
917	Answer the fucking phone.
918	I'm not a fucking machine.
919	It's not my fucking job.
920	Nope.
921	What a nice, fucking bartender.
922	Bullshit, the bastard short-pours.

TED CARELOCK

A Day Off

So you want the day off!

Let's take a moment to look at what you are asking for.

There are 365 days available for work.

There are fifty-two weeks per year,

Of which you already have two days off each weekend,

Leaving 261 days left available for work.

Since you spend sixteen hours each day away from work,

That accounts for 170 days.

There are ninety-one days left available for work.

You spend thirty minutes each day on breaks.

That accounts for twenty-three days each year,

Leaving sixty-eight days available for work.

You spend one hour a day at lunch.

That accounts for another forty-six days per year,

Leaving twenty-two days available for work.

You spend two days per year on sick leave,

Leaving twenty days available for work.

You take nine holidays per year,

Leaving eleven days available for work.

You take ten days of vacation each year,

Leaving one day left available for work.

And no way are you going to take that day off!

When Things Go Wrong

When things go wrong, as they usually will, and your daily road seems
    all uphill,
When funds are low and debts are high, when you try to smile but can
    only cry, and you really feel you'd like to quit,
Don't run to me.
I don't give a shit!

My Yesterday

I have no yesterdays;
Time took them away.
Tomorrow may not be,
But I have today!

Whose Job Is It?

This a story about four people named Everybody, Somebody, Anybody, and Nobody. There was an important job to be done, and Everybody was asked to do it. Everybody was sure Somebody would do it. Anybody could have done it, but Nobody did it. Somebody got angry about that because it was Everybody's job. Everybody thought Anybody could do it, but Nobody realized that Everybody wouldn't do it. It ended up that Everybody blamed Somebody when Nobody did what Anybody could have done.

To Whom It May Concern

The Occupational Safety and Health Administration (OSHA) has determined that the maximum safe-load capacity on my butt is two persons at a time unless I install handrails and safety straps.

As you arrived sixth in line to ride my ass today, please take a number and wait your turn.

Thank you.

I've been beaten,
kicked, lied to,
cussed at,
swindled,
taken advantage of,
and laughed at.

But

the only reason I
hang around this
place is to see
what happens next!

Free Vacation

Sick of living at home with your parents? Stay at our great resort with all the benefits of home without the hassle.

Rikers Island

Amenities include:
Oceanfront view—Free room and board—twenty-four-hour security—Tax-free shopping—Free utilities—Free telephone service—three gourmet meals a day—Free entertainment—Free cable—Free clothing—Personal wake-up service—Free transportation—Diverse religious services

If you qualify, private rooms are available with meals, room service, and private guards.

For your leisure:
Recreation area—Free Nautilus-equipped gym—Fully equipped library—Sexual partners' area available (ask anyone for Bubba)

Educational benefits:
All-expenses paid GED courses—College courses—Life experience credits if you qualify

For more info, dial 911.

Stress

The confusion created
when one's mind overrides
the body's basic desire to
choke the living shit out
of some asshole who
desperately needs it.

TED CARELOCK

What Is a Boss?

When the body was first created,

All the parts wanted to be boss.

The brain said, "Since I control everything and do all the thinking, I should be the boss."

The feet said, "Since I carry man where he wants to go and get him in position to do what the brain wants, I should be boss."

The hands said, "Since I must do all the work and earn all the money to keep the rest of you going, I should be the boss."

The eyes said, "Since I must look out for all of you and tell you where danger lurks, I should be the boss."

And so it went with the heart, the ears, and the lungs. Finally, the asshole spoke up and demanded that it be made boss.

All the other parts laughed and laughed at the idea of an asshole being boss. The asshole got so angry that he locked himself off and refused to function. Soon the brain was feverish, the eyes crossed and ached, the feet were too weak to walk, the hands hung limply at the sides, and the heart and lungs struggled to keep going.

All pleaded with the brain to relent and let the asshole be the boss.

And so it happened. The other parts did all the work, and the asshole just bossed and passed out a lot of shit.

The Moral

You don't have to be a brain to be boss. Just an asshole!

Notice

All employees are requested
to take a bath before
reporting for work.

Since we have to kiss your ass to get you to do anything, we want it to

be nice and clean!

—The Management

Would you be terribly upset
if I asked you to take
your silly-assed problem
down the block?

Thank you

Effective:
New Office Policy

Dress Code:

1) You are advised to come to work dressed according to your salary.

2) If we see you wearing Prada shoes and carrying a Gucci bag, we will assume you are doing well financially and, therefore, do not need a raise.

3) If you dress poorly, you need to learn to manage your money better so that you may buy nicer clothes, and, therefore, you do not need a raise.

4) If you dress just right, you are right where you need to be and, therefore, you do not need a raise.

Sick Days:
We will no longer accept a doctor's statement as proof of sickness. If you are able to go to the doctor, you are able to come to work.

Personal Days:
Each employee will receive 104 personal days a year.
They are called Saturdays and Sundays.

Bereavement Leave:
This is no excuse for missing work. There is nothing you can do for dead friends, relatives, or coworkers. Every effort should be made to have nonemployees attend to the funeral arrangements in your place. In rare cases where employee involvement is necessary, the funeral should be scheduled in the late afternoon. We will be glad to allow you to work through your lunch hour and break and leave one hour early.

Bathroom Breaks:

Entirely too much time is being spent in the toilet. There is now a strict three-minute time limit in the stalls. At the end of three minutes, an alarm will sound, the toilet paper roll will retract, the stall door will open, and a picture will be taken. After your second offense, your picture will be posted on the company bulletin board under the "Chronic Offenders" category. Anyone caught smiling in the picture will be sectioned under the company's mental health policy.

Lunch Break:

*   Skinny people get thirty minutes for lunch as they need to eat more so that they can look healthy.

*   Normal-size people get fifteen minutes for lunch to get a balanced meal to maintain their average figure.

*   Chubby people get five minutes for lunch because that's all the time needed to drink a Slim-Fast.

Thank you for your loyalty to our company. We are here to provide a positive employment experience. Therefore, all questions, comments, concerns, complaints, frustrations, irritations, aggravations, insinuations, allegations, accusations, contemplations, consternation, and input should be directed elsewhere.

The Management
Pass this on to all who are employed!

TED CARELOCK

To Err Is Human ...

But to really foul things up,
you need a computer.

How can you tell
when a salesman
is lying?

His lips move.

Table of Excuses

Please give the excuse by number to save time:

1. That's the way we've always done it.
2. I didn't know you were in a hurry for it.
3. That's not in my department.
4. No one told me to go ahead.
5. I'm waiting for an OK.
6. How did I know this was different?
7. That's her job, not mine.
8. Wait 'til the boss comes back and ask him.
9. I forgot.
10. I didn't think it was very important.
11. I'm so busy I just can't get around to it.
12. I thought I told you.
13. I wasn't hired to do that.

Please!
I can only do
twelve things
at once!

Doing nothing
is very tiring
because you
can't stop and
take a rest.

What Did You Hear?

I know you believe that you understand

what you think I said,

but I am not sure you realize that

what you heard is not what I meant.

Working Here

Working here is like working in a *whorehouse*:
The better you perform, the more they *screw* you!

A Boss Is Like a Diaper ...

Always on your ass and always full of shit!

TED CARELOCK

Warning

My disposition changes without notice.

Lonesome?

Like to meet new people?
Like a change?
Like excitement?
Like a new job?

Just screw up one more time!

Every day
of my life I'm
forced to add
another name to the
list of people
who can just
kiss my ass!

List for Today

_____

_____

_____

Rate Schedule

Answers $1.00

Answers that require thought $2.00

Correct answers $4.00

Dumb looks are still free.

Notice

This department requires no physical fitness program. Everyone gets enough exercise jumping to conclusions, flying off the handle, running down the boss, dodging responsibility, and pushing their luck.

Due to AIDS

Due to the outbreak of AIDS, employees will no longer be permitted to kiss the boss's ass!

My Yesterday

I have no yesterdays.
Time took them away.
Tomorrow may not be,
But I have today!

If

If you can keep your head when all about you
Are losing theirs and blaming it on you,
If you can trust yourself when all men doubt you
But make allowance for their doubting too,
If you can wait and not be tired by waiting,
Or being lied about but don't deal in lies,
Or being hated but don't give way to hating,
And yet don't look too good or talk too wise—

If you can dream and not make dreams your master,
If you can think and not make thoughts your aim,
If you can meet with triumph and disaster
And treat those two imposters just the same,
If you can bear to hear the truth you've spoken
Twisted by knaves to make a trap for fools,
Or watch the things you gave your life to broken,
And stoop and build 'em up with worn-out tools—

If you can make one heap of all your winnings
And risk it on one turn of pitch-and-toss
And lose, and start again at your beginnings
And never breath a word about your loss;
If you can force your heart and nerve and sinew
To serve your turn long after they are gone
And to hold on when there is nothing in you
Except the will which says to them, "Hold on!"—

TED CARELOCK

If you can talk with crowds and keep your virtue
Or walk with kings but not lose the common touch,
If neither foes nor loving friends can hurt you,
If all men count with you but none too much,
If you can fill the unforgiving minute
With sixty seconds' worth of distance run—

Yours is the earth, and everything that's in it.
And, what is more, you'll be a man, my son!

For Lovers

Maybe it's your kiss, your smile,
Your style, or your grace,
But I don't know of anyone under the sun
Who could ever take your place.

And I know as we live to be one hundred
I would never, ever, never, ever
Fall out of love with you.

Something very special happens to me
Each and every time that we touch.
And whenever we have to be apart,
Honey, I miss you, miss you oh, so much.

And as we live to be one hundred I know
I would never, no, not ever, never, never,
Never, naw, never.
I would never, ever, never, ever fall out
Of love with you.

Our love has flourished for these few
Beauty-full years.
And the thirst of our love
Is drenched, quenched, and nourished
By the joy of our tears.

And I know as we live to be one hundred,
I would never, ever, never, ever
Fall out of love with you.

I look forward to the future of our love,
From the foundation of our present
And our past. And I feel sure, secure
That our love will endure.
I know it's gonna last, last, last, and last.

And as we live to be one hundred, I know
I would never, no, no, ever, never, never,
Never, naw, never,
I would never, ever, never, ever fall out
Of love with you.

I would never, never, never
Fall out of love with you
Because I'm certain that you're mine.
You are the only one who can make my
Love light, light up and shine,
And that's why I gladly sign on the
Dotted line; I'm yours, and you're mine.

Thank You for Not Smoking

Cigarette smoke is the residue of your pleasure.
It pollutes the air, contaminates my hair,
And dirties my clothes—not to mention
What it does to my lungs.

This takes place without my consent.

I have a pleasure also; I like a beer now and again.
The residue from my pleasure is urine.
Would you be annoyed if I stood on a chair
Without your consent and pissed on your head?

Thank you for your understanding.

Love Spectrum

"I love you."

There is a much greater motivation than simply my spoken works.

For me to love is to commit myself freely and without reservation. I am sincerely interested in your happiness and well-being. Whatever your needs are, I will try to fulfill them and will bend in my values depending on the importance of your need. If you are lonely and need me, I will be there. If in that loneliness you need to talk, I will listen. If you need to listen, I will talk. If you need the strength of human touch, I will touch you. If you need to be held, I will hold you. I will lie with you if that be your need. If you need fulfillment of the flesh, I will give you that also, but only through my love.

* * *

Love is universal. Love is the movement of life. I have loved a man, a girl, my parent, art, nature, and all things in life I find beautiful. No human being or society has the right to condemn any kind of love I feel or my way of expressing it if I am sincere; sincerity being the honest realization of myself, and there is no hurt or pain intentionally in my life, your life, or anything I touch.

* * *

I want to become a truly loving spirit. Let my words, if I must speak, become the restoration of your soul. But when speech is silent, does a man project the great depth of his sensitivity? When I touch you, kiss you, or hold you, I am saying a thousand words.

Is this the end of this love spectrum? No! Love goes forever.

September 11, 2001

People regularly on their way to their job,
Not knowing that at the end of the day, they would sob.
Everywhere corruption, dust, and smoke.
Everyone's senses were awoke.

People wondering how to get out of the city.
I watched them on TV with such pity.
People were running everywhere,
While all the explosion's particles were in the air.

The people in the city all filled with fear.
Every day, some still shed a tear.
Was this a movie or a show?
Was it possible that some had nowhere to go?

Although our security is very tight,
The war on terrorism will yet be a long fight.
But this is an unbeatable land,
And no matter what they may do, *united we stand!*

—Janine Carelock

September 11, 2001

People regularly on their way to their job,
Not knowing that at the end of the day they would sob.
Everywhere corruption, dust, and smoke.
Everyone's senses were awoke.

The sky was no longer blue.
What could we possibly do?
People running everywhere,
While all the particles were in the air.

The people in the city all filled with fear.
Every day some shed a tear.
The Twin Towers were attacked.
We had no way of knowing; that's a fact.

Our nation is strong.
Although what happened was very wrong,
I will never forget this awful day
When one of New York's famous landmarks went away!

—Janine Carelock

Drummer Boy

(Written with heartfelt love to my dad and uncles.)

You were who I'd become,
        although I wanted to be Roy Rogers,
                and when I turned five,
you let me be Roy Rogers for my
        birthday, and Lynne was Dale Evans.
And all my other cousins and playmates,
they were cowboys and Indians too.
You did that!
        You gave us and enabled us
to have our childhoods;
                children seldom have those anymore.
You were who I'd become.
Though you never put yourselves on
pedestals; if anything,
you stressed that we be better than
        you.
You worked and labored
one, two, and sometimes three jobs
so that yours would have more
than you ever had. That became your ethic.
        You never placed yourselves on pedestals, never!
You just brought your paychecks home
and ate lunches from brown bags,
and warmed dinners up over hot-water pots
                'cause dinner had usually been eaten by
        the time you got home.
And you didn't get to play golf on your
days off 'cause there was always work
for you to do in the house.

You did have fun, though, on
      Saturday nights and Thanksgivings and
        Fourth of Julys. It wasn't much,
          but you had fun;
            and it was fun watching you
              'cause even God
                and us kids
                  knew you deserved it!

You had fun also on
      Christmas mornings,
        watching as we'd enjoy
        all you'd worked yearlong to give.
            You became all the Three Kings,
          and the Little Drummer Boy too!

  "You played your song for Him,"
        and you played your very best.

And now I can play for you,
    —ba rump a
        bump bum—
    'cause you're who I've become.

                  —Teddy Miller (June 1998)

To My Critics

When I'm in a sober mood,
I worry, work, and think.
When I'm in a drunken mood,
I gamble, screw, and drink.
And when my moods are over,
And my time has come to pass,
I hope they bury me upside down,
So the world can kiss my ass!

God bless you!

PHOTOS
AND PRESS

Starlight:
The News Room Staff

Baseball Great Babe Ruth in the club in the 30's.

Thanks everyone for a successful fifth anniversary
celebration last Saturday.

Times Reporter
(Published July 25, 1996)

Miss Vinnie Knight

Cool Jazz in Stadium Shadow

The Newsroom bills itself as a jazz and sports bar, but it's really a one-ring circus—a neighborhood cocktail lounge with free entertainment and a parade of picaresque people perpetually pouring past its portal.

It's what Harlem was like when Harlem was Harlem.

Located at 161st Street and Gerard Avenue, in the shadow of Yankee Stadium, The Newsroom offers poetry readings on Mondays, jam sessions on Sundays and Thursdays, and other events on weekends, with no admission charge and no minimum.

Last Friday the blues and jazz artist Miss Vinnie Knight rocked the room, performing with a guitarist, a bass player and a drummer who looked like Sammy Davis Jr.'s hepcat cousin.

She stalked the floor with the icy hauteur of Nina Simone, the silky sensuality of Carmen McCrae, the haunting vulnerability of Dinah Washington, the inerrant musicality of Ella Fitzgerald and the wacky wit of Millie Jackson.

Miss Vinnie Knight is a star, only the world doesn't know it yet. Raised in Harlem, in the same building where Milton Berle grew up, she now lives in Brooklyn and performs all over—clubs, restaurants, weddings, you name it. She's far more talented than most of the poseurs on MTV, but they've gotten breaks that have yet to come her way.

Would you go see Whitney Houston if she performed at The Newsroom? Then try to catch Miss Vinnie Knight. It's the same thing, only better.

Bronx Cheers

All-out support for the re-election of Mayor David N. Dinkins was given by this prominent group of Bronx residents at a fund-raising reception at the popular News Room Restaurant, 854 Gerard Ave., last Thursday. Participating in the gala pre-election affair were (l–4) Allen Roberts, Ted Carelock, owner of the nightspot; Mrs. Deonie Carelock, Councilmember Wendell Foster, State Senator Joseph Galiber, and Mrs. Allene S. Roberts, who, with her husband, co-hosted the well-attended event.